Amos Ilgenfritz and the Ebb & Flow

Unlock the Power of Cash Flow to Build an Exceptional Business

By **Gregory Brickner**

Published by Olga Press

Olga
PRESS

Amos Ilgenfritz and the Ebb & Flow: Unlock the Power of Cash Flow to Build an Exceptional Business

Copyright © 2020 by Gregory Brickner

10 9 8 7 6 5 4 3 2 1

Olga Press, LLC | olgapress.com | 1-888-886-READ

ISBN: 978-1-7351425-2-4
eISBN: 978-1-7351425-1-7

97GAA

Dedication

To the CFOs and mentors who helped me grow professionally and learn the importance of cash flow—specifically Doug B., Michael S., David H., and Mike G.

Contents

Introduction

What is the most crucial element in business? Most people think of things like sales or profits. The reality is a company can be profitable and also forced to close their doors. Heard the saying "cash is king"? It is more than a management cliche since cash flow is what drives a business. Some entrepreneurs have built huge enterprises without cash flow, but they had access to capital.... this is still cash! For any business to count on financing or capital infusions to stay in business is a dangerous game.

Plain and simple, do not run out of cash. In business, you can run out of just about everything; you can take backorders, crash your website, have the worst day possible, and still recover. Running out of cash is the one thing you can not do under any circumstances. The minute you do, your business is dead.

In this book, I paint a fictional tale of Amos to explain cash flow. If you think you won't be able to relate, give it a chance. Sure, you may have different products and different general ledger accounts, but all business comes down to cash in and cash out. Your company might use different terminology, but I promise that you will gain a new understanding of cash flow, whether you work in a finance/accounting role or as a manager of a business operation.

Over the last twenty years, I have seen how the best businesses have leveraged cash flow to fund their growth, and how the worst companies ignore cash flow to their peril. My career in corporate finance has provided me a front-row seat to see the good, bad, and ugly of cash management in large and small businesses.

The story of Amos Ilgenfritz and his business is an explanation of cash flow for business leaders to make better decisions that impact cash. You can download the financial statements for Ilgenfritz Robotics used in this book at https://amos.fcf.is.

Now let us have some fun together and learn from Amos Ilgenfritz as he explores the ebb and flow of cash flow.

The Cash Crisis

Amos Ilgenfritz is the founder and CEO of Ilgenfritz Robotics. After college, he held several jobs with equipment manufactures. Bored and stifled at work, he began to tinker in his free time and soon had developed a minimum viable product for what was to become Ilgenfritz Robotics Corp. Ilgenfritz Robotics is a leader in its field today and services customers worldwide. Amos grew the business carefully and methodically. He started the business by trialing his simple idea and brought a minimum viable product to market fast. It was cheap and crude, yet he was able to prove the demand for his first robot concept existed.   Amos quickly refined the product to improve upon the MVP and continued to grow sales.

Amos was surprised last week when his banker called and said he was about to max out the line of credit the company had and wanted to know if he wanted to increase the borrowing capacity. The company had an incredible rise in sales in the last six months with the launch of the RX71. This robotic model was a refinement of a previous model but tailored specifically for the agriculture market. A warm reception at the World AG Expo fueled the rise in sales after the market saw the robot's impressive capabilities firsthand. This new model showed off the company's strengths in developing great robotic products. Not just a physical robot, but also the software tools to simplify the use and technical support maximize the client's success. Overall the program has been a win for the company.

This surprise phone call has hit Amos in the gut. He had been through some very tough circumstances as the company grew. In the early days, it never seemed like they could have enough cash, and payroll Fridays always stressed him out. Several years ago, Amos talked to his banker and set up a line of credit to help smooth out cash flow. This move proved fortuitous when sales slumped during the Great Recession. Capital spending from several vital customers dried up, and sales started to fall. To respond, the company pushed intensely into services and software to create a recurring revenue stream around its products. The banker didn't seem worried and suggested that as the company grew, it is normal for the company to need more capacity on the line of credit.

As Amos reflected on the phone call, he kept coming back to a phrase his banker used, "ebb and flow." The banker had said something like "as things ebb and flow" as a way of suggesting it was usual for the company to need a more significant line of credit. Amos continued to ponder this and was perplexed. He asked himself, "How can cash be running out when sales are up significantly, and this is our most profitable model?"

The next day Amos called Jacob, the company Controller, and asked for a copy of his financials. Jacob promptly sent him last month's income statement, statement of cash flow, and balance sheet. Amos began to study the numbers.

What is Cash Flow?

Cash flow refers to the movement and amount of a business's incoming and outgoing money. It is one of the main determinants of a company's financial health. It reflects how much money the business takes in as income compared to the amount it sends out for expenditures.

Positive cash flow reflects a business's capacity to pay off creditors and debts. On the other hand, a negative cash flow indicates that a company is incapable of paying off debts using cash from its operations and will need to find another source of income to compensate for these debts.

Cash flow is crucial in the analysis and evaluation of a business's financial performance. Using a cash flow statement for financial analysis applications, a leader can calculate metrics such as Cash Conversion Ratio and IRR (Internal Rate of Return).

We know that Amos has almost maxed out the short-term line of credit of the company. With this information, we can deduce that the company is consuming lots of cash and has a negative cash flow.

Amos Reviews the Income Statement.

The income statement or statement of profit and loss shows the revenue and expenses of the company. Amos reviewed each line. Revenue in each of the three segments was up as expected, and Amos was proud of the gains the company had made. He thought back to the first sales of the IX2, the very first robot the company sold. He laughed now how the first customer called within hours of receiving the unit to buy a second battery because the charge time was too short. Amos knew the issue was the hastily written code that was consuming power and causing the battery to run dead. The company's products have come along way since then. Today, the customers were buying the units in the dozen to deploy advanced robotic systems that worked together. Sales revenue reflected this behavior and were up significantly as a result.

Amos continued down the page and studied the Cost of Good Sold lines. The figures were more significant than the past because sales had gone up as expected. Here again, though, Amos was proud of the company's performance as the gross margins had increased. The gross margin shows how much the company makes from selling its products before any overhead expenses. The RX71 and its phenomenal margins were making the overall margins of the company shine. The company is also selling software and other services now. It cost almost nothing for the company to install a second or third copy of the software code, so the margins on software are fantastic. Amos thought about the headaches, delays, and what seemed like pure torture to ship the first version of the program. Each sale today only costs the bandwidth for the customer to download the application creating a massive payoff for the company. The company even stopped printing manuals and making CDs with the application, which was a small cost, but today everything is download so it became an unnecessary expense.

Amos sat and reflected on what he learned so far. Sales are up, the cost to make the products is lower per robot, but the expense has risen because sales are up. Thus Amos summarizes, "Our profit from each unit is better than last year, and we are selling more units, yet we have less cash in the bank."

The next section of the income statement has Selling and Administrative Expenses. Amos again is pleased with how well the team has controlled expenses. They have hired a few key staff members to help with the launch of the RX71, yet overall payroll expenses are only slightly up from last year. Sales and marketing expenses are only up somewhat as well. Amos makes a note to commend Anna, the VP of Sales and Marketing, for the excellent performance of increasing sales so dramatically with minor increases in expenses. Amos then reaches the product liability insurance line and warranty expense line, which are both significantly up from last year. He is alarmed and immediately calls Sarah, the VP of Operations.

Amos was intense during his conversation with Sarah, but as usual, she held her own and knew the details. Amos was concerned there were issues with the new RX71 that he did not know about, and it was driving up expenses. To be sure he was in the details, Amos had Sarah send the warranty claim reports. He recalled how to log into the company's ERP software to run analytics on the older product's claims versus the new RX71. Everything Sarah had told him checked out, the warranty claims were better than any product the company had shipped – EVER. Amos then replayed the conversation with Sarah again in his mind. He remembered Sarah saying that she had been arguing with Jacob, the company Controller, over the calculation of warranty and product liability expenses. It was late, so Amos sent Jacob an email to meet first thing in the morning. He knew Jacob might still be working since he was getting ready for a meeting with the bank later in the week. Amos did not believe the company needed the bigger line of credit, but he was going to ask for one to give himself time to figure things out.

Amos continued down the page and finished studying the expenses and reached a line labeled "EBITDA." Amos knew this meant Earnings Before Interest Taxes Depreciation and Amortization. EBITDA is how accountants describe Operating Income. Amos is pleased again to find the company made a healthy profit. Pondering this some more, Amos asks himself, "if the company is profitable, why are we running out of cash… the profit should be cash in the bank?"

Further down the page, Amos reads the small amount of interest the company pays on an equipment loan used to purchase new tooling for the RX71 startup, the depreciation of those assets, and the other equipment the company has. The company bought a new fabrication facility a few years ago, which has significantly increased the depreciation expense. Amos notices the amortization expense is relatively insignificant and recalls the days when the cost was much higher from the startup expenses the company incurred. Nothing pops out to Amos here, but he takes a few notes to talk to Jacob about.

Finally, Amos reaches the net income line of the income statement and smiles at this handsome profit. He knew the company was profitable because Jacob reviews the income statement every month with the leadership team. Once a month, Amos holds a local offsite meeting that takes an entire day for leaders to report on their progress towards company objectives. Jacob does an excellent job of reviewing the margins and profitability indicators. Amos remains perplexed.

The Income Statement and Cash

Amos did a good job reviewing the Income Statement for the company and asked questions to align his understanding of the operations with the financials. Sarah specifically had an item that did not make sense to Amos.

The matching principle of accounting is a crucial point to keep in mind when reviewing the results. Meaning that Jacob and the accounting team are following Generally Accepted Accounting Principles or GAAP when preparing the Income Statement and working hard to keep the expenses associated with the revenue in the same periods. For Ilgenfritz Robotics, this means they record all of the expected costs for each robot when it sells because this is when the company records the revenue. What Amos found with the warranty expense is valid for the entire income statement. The accountants are estimating a future liability for warranty claims and recording it as an expense at the time of sale. The warranty expense increased because sales went up, not because there were more warranty claims. The accounting process creates a reserve fund for future warranty claims that may happen.

Operating income is important because it shows the profit or loss of the business before funding the capital structure of the business. If a company chooses to finance with more or less debt, buy assets, or lease them or is a corporation or sole proprietorship or partnership, these decisions all impact the taxes, depreciation, and amortization lines. By looking at Earnings BEFORE Interest Taxes Depreciation and Amortization, we can see how the business performs regardless of who owns it. Or at least this is how the theory goes.

Since the matching principle is moving expenses around the company from inventory and reserves, we cannot use operating income as an equivalent for cash. The balance sheet captures and details each pile of money as liabilities or assets, depending on the transaction.

Amos Reviews the Balance Sheet

The balance sheet was the second file that Jacob had emailed to Amos. The report was pretty simple for the company, and Amos dove into the first section of Assets. The assets section is split again into current and long-term assets. Current assets are items that can be quickly sold or expected to convert to cash within a year. The company bank accounts, along with accounts receivables and inventory, are current assets. Also listed were prepaid expenses and other current assets. Nothing stood out to Amos, and he did note that inventory and accounts receivables had increased significantly over the prior year. He thought, "I am surprised inventory is not higher to push all these sales out the door." Then jotted a note to review inventory with Sarah and make sure customers are having their orders quickly filled.

Under long-term assets were the usual items that Amos was familiar with, the few buildings the company owned as the equipment and company vehicles. The company had not added to these accounts in the last year, so the only line that had changed was the depreciation.

Moving further down the page, Amos came upon Liabilities. Like the assets section above, current and long-term liabilities divided the total assets into two parts. Current liabilities are debts and obligations the company has that it must pay within the next year. Listed under current liabilities, Amos read accounts payable, accrued payroll, credit cards, and the bank line of credit. All of these were close to the prior year balances except for the line of credit. Amos about fell out of his chair and exclaimed, "Gee Willikers! We've more than tripled the line of credit!"

Under long-term debt, the company held a small mortgage and the equipment loan used to finance the new tooling. Amos again smiled as he knew he was doing the right thing by keeping the company out of debt as much as possible. He prided himself in the frugality he used to steer the company through the Great Recession and knew many companies had failed because they had too much debt.

Amos pulled his calculator from his desk drawer and ran a few quick calculations. He was figuring out the debt ratios that he had always held as crucial operating best practices. The debt to asset levels, quick ratio, and current ratio all looked good. He started to see the day the company could be debt-free, but first, he had to figure out what was causing this cash flow problem.

The final section on the balance sheet Amos read was the Equity section. Under equity, Amos found the capital investments made into the company as well as the retained earnings from prior years and the current year. One other line stuck out, which was the Treasury Stock. Treasury Stock is the stock that the company repurchased from a shareholder, reducing the number of shares outstanding. Treasury Stock is not the stock in another company but buying back the equity in itself. Amos recalled that a few years ago, they bought the shares of his neighbor, Mr. Stoltzfus, to help him when his wife got sick.

The balance sheet made sense to Amos, and nothing struck him as odd. He felt the company was in overall better shape than it had been since he started the firm. Yet something was wrong.

The Balance Sheet and Cash

The balance sheet summarizes the totals of the financial tracking accounts used to monitor the company's activity. Each account is almost like a little pile of money that represents the adjustments to the income statement. Each account tracks the operation of a part of the business. The accounts have monetary balances that create the total but are not like the cash held in a bank account. The balances represent the tracking of money used to run the business. The monitoring of activities around the company is an attempt to create the most accurate financial statements possible. Some of the accounts are real bank accounts and loans. The balance sheet pulls all of the tracking mechanisms and real accounts together to show the company's financial health at a specific point in time.

When the company sells a robot and adds to the warranty expense reserve, it is matching the expense to the sale on the income statement and then adding a liability that is an estimate of the customer's problem that may arise in the future. No cash went out the door. We told the shareholders and anyone that uses the balance sheet that there is a potential for customers to make claims in the future, and the company believes the total of the warranty claims will not exceed this amount. Do they? Only the future knows for sure.

Amos found accrued payroll as a current liability account. The company accountants calculated the payroll cost up to and including the last day of the month. Since the employees are unpaid, this amount is a future debt owed by the company– likely next Friday-- so it becomes a current liability. This process allows the company to matched its expense for the period by recording the payroll cost for the entire month even though it is unpaid.

As you can see, things like sales, payroll, and purchases are continually happening in every company, big and small. The balance sheet is a snapshot in time that shows us what the company looked like at that very moment. Much like a photograph records the water flowing over a waterfall. Immediately before and immediately after the photo, everything changed. The same is true of a balance sheet. It shows us the balances of the accounts at that very moment.

Amos Reviews the Cash Flow Statement

Amos clicks on the last file Jacob had sent, and it is the Cash Flow Statement. The first line is net income, which has the same total from the Income Statement. Amos jokes to himself, "This is always like they took the Balance Sheet and Income Statement and put them in a blender." After net income is an add-back for depreciation, which also matches the Income Statement, then follows a listing of "change in..." lines. Each one has a positive or negative total. Change in accounts receivables, change in accounts payable, change in other assets. The list goes on. The only thing that strikes Amos is the big negative on the line that reads Cash Flow from Operations.

The next section continues the same way and is labeled Cash Flow from Investing and Financing Activities. There is little movement here and shows the repayments made on the mortgage and equipment loan. Then a line labeled net borrowings under the line of credit, there is the significant increase we saw on the balance sheet.

Finally, at the end of the report is a modest change in cash during the year and increase in total ending cash. The total net change matches the difference in the checking account balance. One of the staff accountants sent this number to Amos every day, and Amos thought he was monitoring the company's cash position. It never really seemed to move much, and he realizes he practically ignores it now.

The Statement of Cash Flow and Cash

The statement of cash flow shows the real movement of cash in the company by removing the accounting functions that distort cash on the income statement. Even though the wording and organization of the Statement of Cash Flow can make the report's interpretation difficult, it is an accurate picture of the cash in the company.

Amos Meets with Jacob

As planned, Amos meets with Jacob first thing in the morning. Jacob is well prepared and has printed off the financial statements he sent Amos as well as a few other reports to share. The meeting goes well, and they discuss the notes and questions Amos made as he reviewed the financial statements.

Jacob confirmed the warranty expense accrual and explained how he is using guidance from the local accounting firm to perform the calculations. They dug into the increase in the line of credit. One of the additional reports Jacob provided showed the trended balance sheet. The trended balance sheet was convenient, and Amos could now see why the banker called it an "Ebb and Flow." It seemed that every quarter the line of credit would slowly creep up and subsequently decline, only to creep back up again. The trend line was upwards for sure but not the vertical climb that Amos had feared. Cash was moving through the business, and the business was profitable, but growth was consuming cash as fast as the company would earn it. Jacob had prepared an analysis using Anna's sales projections that showed the company would run out of money in about seven months if the bank agreed to double the credit line.

Amos was appreciative of Jacob's efforts and walked away from the meeting feeling the stress of the challenge and knowing that something else was wrong. "If I do not fix this, the company will be profitable, growing, and broke." Amos thought.

Amos called a special leadership team meeting to review the company's financial performance. He knew he needed all of the brainpower and talent his team had.

Financial Statements
of Ilgenfritz Robotics Corp.

Income Statement
Ilgenfritz Robotics Corp.
Period Ending Dec. 31, 2019

	2019	2018	Variance ($)	Variance (%)
1 Revenue				
2 Net Product Sales	46,821,444	38,393,584	8,427,860	22.0%
3 Net Service Sales	7,572,959	6,815,663	757,296	11.1%
4 Other Revenue	337,271	340,644	(3,373)	-1.0%
5 Total Revenue	54,731,674	45,549,891	9,181,783	20.2%
6 Cost of Sales				
7 Product Cost	21,069,650	18,428,920	(2,640,729)	-14.3%
8 Service Cost	3,937,939	3,475,988	(461,950)	-13.3%
9 Total Cost of Sales	25,007,588	21,904,909	(3,102,680)	-14.2%
10 Total Gross Profit	29,724,086	23,644,982	6,079,103	25.7%
11 Operating Expenses				
12 Salaries, Wages & Benefits	14,609,403	12,915,585	(1,693,818)	-13.1%
13 Selling & Marketing	2,838,317	2,166,167	(672,150)	-31.0%
14 Research & Development	1,941,429	1,525,307	(416,122)	-27.3%
15 Fulfillment & Operations	1,954,531	2,525,552	571,021	22.6%
16 Other Operating Items	601,498	341,851	(259,647)	-76.0%
17 General & Administrative	2,092,891	2,648,072	555,181	21.0%
18 Total Operating Expenses	24,038,069	22,122,534	1,915,535	8.7%
19 Operating Income (EBITDA)	5,686,017	1,522,448	4,163,568	273.5%
20 Depreciation	142,314	135,198	7,116	5.3%
21 Amortization	1,861	2,410	(549)	-22.8%
22 Interest Expense	124,557	130,120	(5,563)	-4.3%
23 Provision for Income Taxes	1,819,525	411,061	1,408,464	342.6%
24 Net Income	3,597,759	843,659	2,754,100	326.4%

Unaudited - For Management Use Only

Balance Sheet

Ilgenfritz Robotics Corp.

Period Ending Dec. 31, 2019

	2019	2018
1 Assets		
2 Current Assets		
3 Cash & Cash Equivilents	212,436	224,618
4 Accounts Receivable, net	12,345,390	6,815,663
5 Inventories	7,224,393	5,815,663
6 Other Current Assets	2,338,634	340,644
7 Total Current Assets	22,120,853	13,196,588
8 Non-Current Assets		
9 Intellectual Property	1,618,549	1,107,817
10 Property, Plant, & Equipment, net	32,064,066	31,978,832
11 Other Non-Current Assets	2,180,903	2,619,988
12 Total Non-Current Assets	35,863,518	35,706,637
13 Total Assets	57,984,371	48,903,225
14 Liabilities & Shareholder Equity		
15 Current Liabilities		
16 Accounts Payable	2,809,807	2,009,168
17 Other Current Liabilities	1,823,819	1,812,378
18 Line of Credit	5,441,646	1,464,514
19 Current Portion of Long-Term Debt	2,026,422	1,975,377
20 Total Current Liabilities	12,101,694	7,261,437
21 Non-Current Liabilities		
22 Facility Mortgage	10,252,737	11,130,371
23 Equipment Loan	2,337,450	2,414,095
24 Other Non-Current Liabilities	2,521,722	924,313
25 Total Non-Current Liabilities	15,111,909	14,468,779
26 Total Liabilities	27,213,603	21,730,216
26 Shareholder Equity		
27 Common Stock & Paid In Capital	10,000,000	10,000,000
28 Treasury Stock	(2,000,000)	(2,000,000)
29 Retained Earnings	19,173,009	18,329,350
30 Current Retained Earnings	3,597,759	843,659
31 Total Shareholder Equity	30,770,768	27,173,009
32 Total Liabilities & Shareholder Equity	57,984,371	48,903,225

Unaudited - For Management Use Only

Cash Flow Statement
Ilgenfritz Robotics Corp.
Period Ending Dec. 31, 2019

	2019	2018
1 Cash, cash equivalents, beginning balances	224,618	194,593
2 Operating Activities		
3 Net Income	3,597,759	843,659
4 Adjustments to reconcile net income to cash generated by operating activities:		
5 Depreciation	142,314	135,198
6 Amortization	1,861	2,410
7 Changes in operating assets and liabilities:		
8 Accounts Receivable, net	(5,529,727)	400,281
9 Inventories	(1,408,730)	(866,534)
10 Other Assets & Liabilities	49,945	1,845,194
11 Accounts Payable	800,639	94,029
12 Cash generated by operating activities	(2,345,938)	2,454,237
13 Investing Activities		
14 Payments to acquire property and equipment	(227,548)	(18,916,147)
15 Payments to acquire intelectual property	(512,593)	(46,723)
16 Cash generated (used) by Investing Activities	(740,142)	(18,962,870)
17 Financing Activities		
18 Line of Credit	3,977,132	857,905
19 Current Portion of Long-Term Debt	51,045	1,604,994
20 Facility Mortgage	(877,634)	10,179,058
21 Equipment Loan	(76,645)	1,896,701
22 Proceeds from issuance of common stock	-	4,000,000
23 Repurchase of Common Stock	-	(2,000,000)
24 Cash generated (used) by Financing Activities	3,073,898	16,538,658
25 Net increase (decrease) in cash and cash equivalents	(12,182)	30,025
26 Cash, cash equivalents, ending balances	212,436	224,618

Unaudited - For Management Use Only

You can download the financial statements for Ilgenfritz Robotics used in this book at https://amos.fcf.is.

The Movement of Cash

Amos was preparing for the team meeting he called and began to review the company's operations. He started by breaking down every action the company took and the impact on cash.

What is Cash

Amos realized we say "cash" a lot, but what is cash? He remembered sometimes the accountants would say "near cash." He made a list:

1. Money in our pocket
2. Cash can also be things that can be turned into cash very quickly such as
   a. Checking account balance
   b. Savings account balance
   c. Our money market account

Amos thought about it a bit more and decided a pot of gold coins is not cash. It is an asset since the gold would need to be converted to dollars to be useful paying bills or payroll.

Then Amos thinks about the transactions the company has and begins to sketch the movements that happen with each.

The Company Buys a Good or Service

The company receives

Goods

The company gives

Cash

Often, the company does not pay for the item immediately. It waits and pays an invoice, which looks like this:

The company receives

Goods

The company gives

A purchase order

The purchase order is accounts payable on the balance sheet. Invoices arrive for things like electricity, trash, and other services provided to the company. These look almost the same:

The company receives

> Services

The company gives

> 30 day promise to pay

When the company pays its bills, it then looks like this:

The company receives

> Invoices

The company gives

> A Check (cash)

Amos considers this for a minute. The company does not pay for services or the goods received at the time of delivery. Instead, the company pays an invoice in many cases 30 - 45 days later.

The Company Sells Goods or Services

Amos reverses the situation and thinks about the same transactions when Ilgenfritz Robotics sells to its customers.

In some cases, the customer pays immediately.

The company receives

> Cash

The company gives

> Goods

Often, the customer does not pay for the item immediately. It waits and pays an invoice, which looks like this:

The company receives

> A purchase order

The company gives

> Goods

The purchase order received from the customer is an accounts receivable on the balance sheet and a sale on the income statement. The company invoices the customer for the merchandise. When the customer pays based on the terms of the invoice, the transaction looks like this:

The company receives

```
Check (cash)
```

The company gives

```
Invoice
```

The accounts receivable balance is then reduced for the customer. Some customers may not pay us on time, or we may have agreed to longer payment terms for special customers.

When a customer does not pay the money that is owed to the company, it is expensed to the income statement as bad debt. This process corrects the accounts receivable balance.

Amos considers this further and notes that at this point, the Ilgenfritz Robotics will have recorded the sale; the revenue and associated profit will be on the income statement, but the balance sheet will show accounts receivable, not cash.

"This is a great example of why profit is not the same thing as cash," says Amos.

Inventory

The company buys inventory in various forms. Sometimes it buys raw materials that are used to make the robots. This inventory is called raw material inventory on the balance sheet. Then the metal and plastic are worked by the skilled craftsmen of the company and show up as work-in-process inventory on the balance sheet. When the robots are finished, the final product is placed in finished goods inventory on the balance sheet. Finally, sometimes we buy goods from other suppliers to resell them to our customers. These goods are also in the inventory totals on the balance sheet.

Amos ponders all of the forms of inventory on the balance sheet and realizes the cash flow is the same, just the amounts and how it reaches the inventory vary. He sketches the inventory cash flow like this:

The company receives

Goods and Labor

The company gives

Cash

When the company receives the goods or materials that are used to build the robots, the cash follows the same flow as any other good or service noted above. For the inventory the company produces, the direct labor is added to the value of the robot as it moves through production. Amos says, "This is payroll dollars, held on the balance sheet in the form of inventory!"

When the robot is sold, the total value of the robot is moved to the income statement as the Cost of Goods Sold expense. All of the labor, parts, materials, and any other expenses are added into the final value of the robot. The company hopes to sell the robot for more than this amount, but the selling price never impacts the total expenses of the inventory.

Loan Financing

Amos knows the company can go to the bank and get a loan to pay the bills, and it looks like this:

The company receives

> Cash

The company gives

> A promise to repay

When we pay back the loan, this is cash out and looks like this.

The company receives

> Payment Request

The company gives

> Cash

Equity Investment

An investor could buy the company's stock and provide an equity investment into the company. Selling equity would look like:

The company receives

> Cash

The company gives

> Company Stock

Then if the company repurchases the stock from the investor, it shows up on the balance sheet as Treasury Stock. The transaction looks like this:

The company receives

> Company Stock

The company gives

> Cash

When the company rewards its shareholders for taking the risk of their investment, it pays a dividend. Dividends looks like this:

The company receives

Shareholder Goodwill

The company gives

Cash

Buying Buildings and Other Expensive Stuff

Amos thinks about other transactions the company has done recently and recalls the new facility and the equipment for the RX71. Buildings, cars, and equipment all have a longer useable life and are not recorded as an expense on the income statement during the month that they are purchased. It would be silly to show a $40,000 cost because the company bought a new pickup truck that is used for several years. Amos recalls that the accounting firm the company uses provides Jacob with an IRS schedule that lists the useful life of everything imaginable. He laughs as he remembers it even list the useful life for 'breeding pigs,' although this value is undoubtedly relevant to the new agricultural customers the company has. The purchase amount is then split based on the expected useful number of months. A vehicle should have a useful life of five years, so every month, 1/60th of the purchase price is recorded as depreciation expense. This procedure moves the cost of the vehicle from the balance sheet and to the income statement.

When the company buys an asset, the transactions look like this:

The company receives

Equipment

The company gives

Cash

Then the cash impact of depreciation is:

Amos quickly scribbles it out. Depreciation is not a cash event. The cash flow happens when acquiring the asset, not during the depreciation period. We might get a loan to buy the building, car, or equipment, and we would have the same cash flow as noted under loans.

Taxes

Amos realizes he cannot forget about taxes. Taxes on the profits of the business is a cash outflow.

The company receives

Tax Notice

The company gives

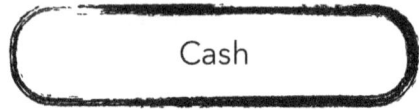

```
┌─────────────────────────────────┐
│                                 │
│              Cash               │
│                                 │
└─────────────────────────────────┘
```

Positive and Negative Cash Flow

Amos believes he has covered all of the transactions the company could have. He then contemplates what all of these transactions together mean.

All of these events of cash coming in and cash going out is what we call cash flow.

When more cash comes in than goes out, we have a positive cash flow.

When more cash is going out than coming in, we have a negative cash flow.

Amos has an idea how to explain this to his team and help them become better business leaders by focusing on cash flow and the company's profit performance.

Translating Results to Cash

The management team of Ilgenfritz Robotics is a small and close group. Amos had picked and sought out each of them based on their stellar performance. He recruited each VP away from their existing position and convinced them to work for the company. Now, the company could fail because they did too good of a job, and the company ran out of cash. Amos was dreading the idea of layoffs, plant closures, and forced pay reductions. He was betting everything on the talent he had assembled.

Amos was not about to leave anything up to chance. He had worked long hours in the last few days to understand the cash situation of the company. Just a week ago, his long-time banker had called and asked if he wanted to increase the borrowing capacity on the line of credit. This call had caught Amos by surprise and sent him reeling. The idea that he nearly maxed out the existing credit line was unthinkable. He had thought the days of cash flow issues were long behind him.

Today, cash flow was the focus of a special meeting he called with his leadership team, and it was time to present his findings.

Amos quickly brought the team up to speed and reviewed the events of the last week. He had spoken to each one individually beforehand and wanted to be sure he had not missed anything, so he retold the story. Amos believes in full transparency with his leadership team and knows it is the only way they can help the company.

Before he could continue, Anna jumped right in and asked, "How can the company be struggling when our profit is through the roof. My team has been smashing our sales targets?" Anna is the VP of Sales, and her team has been doing a great job driving sales of the new RX71 model robot. Sarah piled on and directed to Jacob, "Is there something wrong with the financials you have been giving us Jacob? I know the warranty expense is fishy." Sarah is the VP of Operations and has been arguing with Jacob over the warranty reserve calculation used in accordance to accounting rules. Before the meeting turned into an attack on Jacob, the company Controller, Amos re-focused the group. Amos stated to the group, "Jacob is doing a great job for us, and all of our annual audits have confirmed the high-quality work he does." He continued, "this is why we are meeting today, so we can learn how to translate the profit of the Company into the cash that it yields."

Amos began to explain to the group how the income statement has reserves, accruals, amortizations, and other accounting entries that are correct but do not represent the company's cash. The income statement describes the profit made from selling the units during the month. The balance sheet shows us at a snapshot in time the assets, liabilities, and equity of the company. Finally, the statement of cash flow presents the movement of cash through the company during the month. Jacob snuck in a quick jab "That's right, the statement of cash flow shows you exactly where the problem is, and it is not my numbers." Clearly, Jacob was still ruminating on the grief he took, so Amos settled things down and moved on.

Amos explained that the team needed a way to see how their actions impacted not just the profit, but also the cash flow of the company. Each manager has to have both reference points in their mind when making decisions. Profit is good, but not if it puts the company at risk.

Oliver, the VP of HR, added, "Let me make sure I understand what you are saying; I may not want to prepay for next year's college job fair because the discount may not be worth letting go of our cash, so far in advance?" Amos could see the group coming together again. "That is right, and I'm going to share with you how we will know," said Amos.

Defining Performance

Since Amos started the company, he has focused on more than just the profit the company makes. He uses the work that the robots perform as a benchmark to the success of the company. Joules is the measurement of work in physics. Technically a joule is the energy measurement to move a newton one meter. Amos describes it to his team as lifting an apple. The company's robots move and do work for customers making life better for the planet.

As a child, Amos was fascinated by the rockets that sent a man to the moon. Duplicating the force of a Saturn V rocket has been the goal Amos has focused his management team on. The Saturn V rocket produced twelve trillion joules to send astronauts into orbit. Amos tracks the effort of all of the robots to measure how much work they are doing and believes the company will achieve success when the robots perform an equal twelve trillion joules of work.

Being obsessed with the robots' work made Amos question the company's performance and how to define it. Realizing the robots did work is one thing, but what about the company itself. Amos shared with his team the Cash Performance Report. This report distills all of the movement that is happening between the Income Statement, Balance Sheet, and Cash Flow Statement into one Net Cash Gain result.

On the first day of the month, the company turned on the lights, then shut them off on the last day of the month. The company's joules counter went up, but is that it? Amos knew a lot of effort occurred in the company during the month. Sales were booked, bills were paid, and the customer's goals were achieved. After all of the initiative, work, turmoil, angst, and success during the month, did we end with more cash? If not, why? The Cash Performance Report illustrates where everything went and how well the company performed to turn its efforts into cash in the bank.

This message seemed to resonate with the team, so Amos used his momentum to press into the details. Amos passed out each of the three financial statements along with the Cash Performance Report.

Cash From Sales

Cash from sales is the first section of the report. The opening lines duplicate the revenue lines from the income statement. For Ilgenfritz Robotics, this is the Net Product Sales, Net Service Sales, and Other Revenue lines. Then there is a new line added labeled cash from (lending to) customers.

Anna speaks up, "I've been asking for customer financing for years, so I know we are not lending to our customers." Amos smiles and states, "Yet here we see Anna that without an actual financing program, we are lending to our customer in large sums."

The adjustment to revenue is the change in cash for accounts receivables outstanding or invoices that the customers have not yet paid. When a customer does not pay the invoice for the products they have received right away, the effect is that the company has lent them the money. Many companies naturally expect customers to take thirty to forty-five days to pay an invoice. Sometimes special terms are agreed to, and the customer has ninety-days or even six months to pay the invoice. By making this adjustment, we can see what the total cash in-flow was to the company.

The Cash From Sales total could exceed the Revenue line from the income statement if the total accounts receivables balance declined due to customer payments. As the team contemplated its meaning, Jacob pointed out, "The adjustment Amos is making to sales is the change in AR from the Statement of Cash Flows." Anna adds, "Thank you, Jacob. It also does not matter how many sales invoices we send, we do not make any money until we get paid."

As Amos reviews the results with the team, it becomes critically apparent that most of the company's increase in sales went into accounts receivables as extended payment terms in the fourth quarter.

The report illustrates in a chart the difference between Cash From Sales and Net Revenue over time. Amos calls attention to the trend and how the two were very similar until the most recent year when accounts receivable balances ballooned.

Gross Cash Gain

Gross Cash Gain is the second total on the Cash Performance Report. The total is the cash equivalent to the gross income from the income statement. Included here is the typical cost of goods and services sold lines from the income statement, with an adjustment for cash activity from the statement of cash flow. Inventory is a significant cash activity related to the cost of sales. The second cash adjustment is for accounts payable tied explicitly to the cost of sales vendors. Amos explains, "I had Jacob isolate the vendors that provide the raw materials, services, and other inputs into selling our robots from the total accounts payable balance." Jacob added, "I was sure to save the report, so it is effortless to run going forward."

After studying the report, Sarah pointed out that the inventory changes the company made consumed a lot of cash flow. Amos agreed and explained, "Think of inventory as cash on the shelf." The team decided to review the inventory changes to determine what will happen in the future as sales continue to grow.

Inventory is a buffer that helps protect the company from vendor disruptions and ensures the company can provide excellent service to the customer. Sarah said, "The new RX71 ramp-up had us busy redoing service kits for key customers." It makes little sense to lose sales due to a lack of inventory if the inventory cost is low enough. At the same time, inventory is a risk since it can become obsolete, be damaged, or even stolen. Balancing these factors together is a crucial consideration of management.

Gross Cash Gain and Gross Profits are illustrated together on the report as a graph with trends over time. This graph provides a visual reference to see how the two correlate. The change in inventory levels in the current year draws your attention to the wide divergence.

Oliver asks, "Does this tell us that the P&L is lying to us about how much profit we made?" Amos explains to the team that the Income Statement correctly does its job and provides an accounting of the profit the company earned by selling its products. With the Cash Performance Report, we are analyzing the cash that happened at the same time as those sales. "Once the customers pay us, and if we reduce or stop buying additional inventory, then we will have the cash that the income statement says we should have," Amos explained.

Amos is proud of the team as they begin to pull together. The income statement is correct and shows how much profit the company made in the period. At the same time, profit does not mean cash in the bank. With the cash performance report, they can see the interaction between the income statement, balance sheet, and cash flow statement. Anna adds, "We can manage both profitability as well as the cash."

Operating Expenses

The third section of the Cash Performance Report is the Operating Expense group. Again the report duplicates the operating expense lines from the income statement and continues with the cash adjustments from the statement of cash flow. Here we add the balance of the accounts payable cash flow that is related to non-trade payables. Then a valuable addition is made for the cash spent on capital expenditures.

Capital expenditures are sometimes called "Cap-Ex" (pronounced cap x) and is money spent on buying assets used in the business like machines, computers, buildings, and factories. Capital expenditures are the use of cash placed back to work inside the operations to fuel future growth. The company could buy new production machines so it can increase profits in the future. The company builds new factories so it can produce more products and increase profits in the future. Sometimes a certain amount of capital investment is required just to keep the current sales volume the same. A new service truck might need to be purchased to replace an old and worn out truck. The new truck will not increase sales since the truck will continue servicing the same customers. Yet, not buying a new truck will cause a drop in sales when the old truck breaks down. These capital expenditures are a significant use of cash but only show up on the balance sheet as an asset and depreciate the asset's life to the income statement.

Free Cash Flow

Amos is excited as the energy among the team is growing. He draws everyone's attention to his favorite line on the report, Free Cash Flow. Free Cash Flow is the measurement of company performance that Amos wants his management team to focus on going forward. A company that has a robust Free Cash Flow is demonstrating the ability to purchase assets such as property, equipment, and other significant investments from the operating cash flow. Strong free cash flow is how the company creates the ability to self fund the cash needed to grow. The company can use the Free Cash Flow to expand operations, hire additional employees, and invest in other assets to increase future profits. If management decided that the company's investment opportunities were not lucrative enough, they could use the cash to acquire another business or provide a dividend to the shareholders.

Sarah points out "Had our inventory been using as much cash as it is right now, we would have never been able to fund the RX71 development." Sarah is spot on, and Amos is thrilled. Amos had strategically planned several years ago to use the Free Cash Flow of the company to develop the RX71. At the time, some of the shareholders felt the company would be better off to pay a dividend and extract as much cash as possible from the existing product line. Amos was focused on the long-term growth of the company to achieve his personal goal of 12 trillion joules. The existing product line was not going to put the company in a position to hit this goal.

Free Cash Flow is a quality indicator of the company's overall performance because it removes the accounting adjustments and reflects the increase or decrease in cash during the month or year after capital expenditures. Amos points out that the measurement is after capital expenditure and sometimes gets distorted by significant capital investments. Last year the company bought a new factory and had a massive drop in Free Cash Flow.

Amos reviews the trended graph on the Cash Performance Report that compares Free Cash Flow and EBITDA with the team. The sudden dip in Free Cash Flow last year is recovered almost entirely this year. The consistent trend of a positive and growing Free Cash Flow is what the company wants to have on the chart. A positive Free Cash Flow trend provides the company options when needing to raising capital, acquire another business, or even attract other investors to buy the company.

Free Cash Flow measurements should always be compared to peers within the same business line or industry because of the fluctuations in capital expenditures. If a company is generating excessively high Free Cash Flow, it could indicate the company is not making the needed investments back into the business to ensure future growth or possibly to merely keep pace.

Negative Free Cash flow is not always an immediate cause for alarm. As with Ilgenfritz Robotics, the company had a dramatic decline in Free Cash Flow because of the factory purchase.

Digging deeper will help reveal the cause of the fall. Investments in future growth can be okay unless the trend never seems to recover. The takeaway is the consistency over a long-term time horizon. It is possible that a prior growth strategy has not paid off and is now a negative drain on the company.

Using Free Cash Flow as the benchmark for performance keeps leaders focused on the health of the company. Having a substantial amount of cash flow says the company has plenty of money to pay the bills, with enough left over to pay off debt and potentially distribute to investors.

Capital Structure

The capital structure of the company is unique to the business strategy of the owners of the company. Each owner decides if they prefer to finance the company with more debt and less equity or maybe only equity and no debt. The founders choose the legal form of the company at startup. They select among being a proprietorship, partnership, a corporation, or one of the variations some states offer. Choosing the capital structure is more about accomplishing the owner's goals and less about the type of industry of the company. The owners may decide to change the capital structure to achieve new goals they may have.

Amos started Ilgenfritz Robotics and incorporated the company to sell stock and receive the cash needed to grow the business. He then decided to use a mix of both debts from banks and the equity investment from the stock sales to create the company's capital structure.

On the Cash Performance Report, we can see the outcome of these decisions on cash flow. By having debt, the company must pay interest to its lenders which becomes an expense of the company. As a corporation, the company pays business taxes to federal, state, and local governments in various forms. The company may increase or decrease its debt, and the resulting change is labeled "net borrowings." An increase in debt is a source of cash, and paying debt becomes a use of cash. As a corporation, Ilgenfritz Robotics can sell an ownership interest in the form of stock to receive cash and may buy back the stock from the investors from time to time, which would be a use of cash. Investors could anticipate a dividend, which rewards them for the risk they have taken by investing in the company. Dividends are a use of cash and depend on the strategy of the company.

Net Cash Gain

The net cash gain is precisely equal to the change cash for the period reported. The difference between the cash at the beginning of the month versus the total cash at month-end becomes the net cash gain. Cash is the checking accounts, savings accounts, and any other bank accounts that hold cash or "near-cash" by the business. A certificate of deposit is a particular savings option a bank offers, which is a form of "near cash."

The total net cash gain should match the net increase or decrease in cash line from the statement of cash flows.

Metrics

Oliver shouted, "Wait a minute; we are out of money in two weeks!" Amos showed the team the right column of the Cash Performance Report, and Oliver gasped as he read it. "Only if our customers stop paying us," Jacob replied.

The right side of the Cash Performance Report has five key performance metrics for the company. Each company is unique and may track slightly different metrics that are meaningful to their business.

The Five KPI Metrics:
1. **Strength.** The selected metric should show the overall health of the company. Amos picked Days Cash Available, which is the cash the company has plus available borrowing capacity divided by the daily expense burn of the company.

2. **Growth.** This metric measures the rate the company is expanding sales. As long as we have inflation, any company that is not growing is shrinking. To measure growth Amos used Cash Sales Growth. Not just sales growth but the growth in cash flow from sales. Focusing on Cash Sales Growth is essential for the company since AR collections have been weak.

3. **Speed.** How fast is the company generating cash? The Cash Cycle metric shows the number of days cash is locked up in the company. The measurement starts at the initial inventory purchase and ends when the customer pays the invoice. The Cash Cycle is the cash stopwatch for the business.

4. **Performance.** Amos selected Free Cash Flow margin as the performance metric of the company. Free Cash Flow is often best viewed over a long-term trend because of capital purchases. He intentionally wants everyone on the team to think about the cash generated from every sale. Inventory and AR are consuming the cash of the company, so every sales transaction is decreasing the cash available to run the company. Amos knows that

measurements drive action, and he needs immediate action.

5. **Fuel.** The fifth metric is cash fuel to grow the company. A business that is generating steady free cash flow can self-fund its growth. Amos is using the Internal Growth Rate of the company as this metric.

Internal Growth Rate

Anna spoke up, "Amos, I love what you have shown us here. This process makes sense to me until you got to Internal Growth Rate. I somehow got lost on the last box." Amos smiled and looked around the room to see the rest of the team nodding in agreement with Anna.

Amos loves the Internal Growth Rate metric and was happy to dive deeper into its meaning for the team. "How fast can our company afford to grow?" Amos asked. The team stared back blankly. Jacob spoke up, "Something less than our current rate for sure." Amos laughed and said, "Exactly, we cannot afford to keep growing at our current rate, and the internal growth rate shows us this."

Amos took the team back to the income statement and pointed out the impressive 20.2% year over year revenue growth the company achieved last year. He explained that this is why the company is running out of cash. The company's internal growth rate is 6.6%. External sources of cash must fund anything beyond 6.6% growth. When the company started, he raised money from investors to pay for the inventory and overhead as the company launched. These investments help the company earn sales, which then paid for new purchases of inventory. This churn is a normal process that every business figures out when it starts. The company has moved well past its startup phase and is now growing sales organically. Internally funding growth means the company can use the profit from prior sales to buy the services, inventory, and overhead expenses needed to create new sales. "This cycle works until sales growth exceeds the capacity of the current investment," Amos said. Amos went on to explain that once the company exceeds this organic capacity to grow sales, then the company must seek external sources of cash. These external sources might be from debt or selling equity in the business. "Essentially, we have gone full circle, and we are back in startup mode?" Sarah questioned. "Only if we allow ourselves to be," Amos responded.

The performance on the other metrics ends up determining the outcome of the final metric. With cash tied up in an extended operating cash cycle - the speed metric - the business cannot grow. With cash tied up in accounts receivable, causing a lower than expected cash sales growth - the growth metric - the company cannot grow. Higher inventories, bad accounts receivables, higher expenses, and weak cash management are all coming together to create a negative free cash flow margin - the performance metric - and the business cannot grow. With such dire cash performance, the company has sixteen days of cash available - the strength metric - and one major hiccup from a customer payment could cause a horrific outcome so the business cannot grow.

"It is all fixable; this is the good news!" Amos shouted to the team. He could see that the group was feeling a bit dejected by the matter of fact performance metrics. "We can fix it now that you are focused on the metrics," Amos continued. He also drew their attention to the company targets and benchmarks that appear with each metric. The company's strategic plan sets the target, and the benchmark is the actual performance of five publicly traded industry peers.

The design of the metrics Amos selected provides the team

with practical insights into how efficient the business is operating and how each decision impacts the organization's health. Each leader can use the Cash Performance Report to determine how they are contributing to the company's success. The metrics are not independent measurements, but integrated cogs in the movement of cash within the company.

"Now you can see as I do, the ebb and flow of cash in our company," Amos stated with a smile. Cash is always moving in the company.

Amos declared it was time for lunch. When they return from lunch, they begin to come up with ideas to improve cash flow and improve the company's cash performance.

Cash Performance Report of Ilgenfritz Robotics Corp.

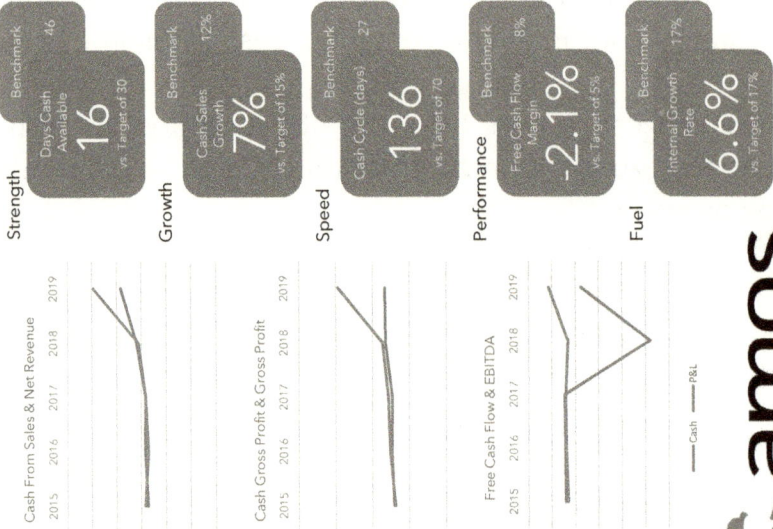

Strength

Days Cash Available — **16** — vs. Target of 30 — Benchmark 46

Growth

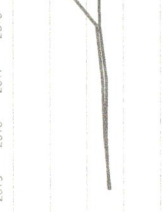

Cash Sales Growth — **7%** — vs. Target of 15% — Benchmark 12%

Speed

Cash Cycle (days) — **136** — vs. Target of 70 — Benchmark 27

Performance

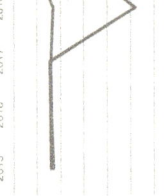

Free Cash Flow Margin — **-2.1%** — vs. Target of 5% — Benchmark 8%

Fuel

Internal Growth Rate — **6.6%** — vs. Target of 17% — Benchmark 17%

Benchmark Target based on performance of 5 Robotics Peers

www.askamos.io | www.fcf.ts

Cash From Sales & Net Revenue

Cash Gross Profit & Gross Profit

Free Cash Flow & EBITDA

— Cash — P&L

Cash Performance Report
Ilgenfritz Robotics Corp.
Dec. 31, 2019 Annual Results

	2019	2018	Variance ($)	Variance (%)
Revenue				
2 Net Product Sales	46,821,444	38,393,584	8,427,860	22.0%
3 Net Service Sales	7,572,959	6,815,663	757,296	11.1%
4 Other Revenue	337,271	340,644	(3,373)	-1.0%
5 Cash from (lending to) customers	(5,529,727)	400,281	(5,930,008)	-1481.5%
6 Cash From Sales	49,201,947	45,950,172	3,251,775	7.1%
7 Cost of Sales				
8 Product Cost	(21,069,650)	(18,428,920)	(2,640,729)	14.3%
9 Service Cost	(3,937,939)	(3,475,988)	(461,950)	13.3%
10 Cash from (used by) Inventory	(1,408,730)	(866,534)	(542,196)	62.6%
11 Cash from (used by) Trade Vendors	520,415	61,119	459,296	751.5%
10 Cash Production Cost	(25,895,903)	(22,710,323)	(3,185,580)	14.0%
11 Gross Cash Gain	23,306,044	23,239,848	66,196	0.3%
12 Operating Expenses				
13 Salaries, Wages & Benefits	(14,609,403)	(12,915,585)	(1,693,818)	13.1%
14 Selling & Marketing	(2,838,317)	(2,166,167)	(672,150)	31.0%
15 Research & Development	(1,941,429)	(1,525,307)	(416,122)	27.3%
16 Fulfillment & Operations	(1,954,531)	(2,525,552)	571,021	-22.6%
17 Other Operating Items	(601,498)	(341,851)	(259,647)	76.0%
18 General & Administrative	(2,092,891)	(2,648,072)	555,181	-21.0%
19 Cash from (used by) Operating Activities	49,945	1,845,194	(1,795,249)	-97.3%
20 Cash from (used by) non-Trade Vendors	280,224	32,910	247,313	751.5%
21 Cash from (used by) Capital Expenditures	(740,142)	(18,962,870)	18,222,728	-96.1%
22 Total Cash Operating Expenses	(24,448,042)	(39,207,300)	14,759,258	-37.6%
23 Free Cash Flow	(1,141,998)	(15,967,452)	14,825,454	92.8%
24 Free Cash Flow Margin	-2.09%	-35.05%	32.97%	94.0%
25 Capital Structure				
26 Interest Expense	(124,557)	(130,120)	5,563	-4.3%
27 Provision for Income Taxes	(1,819,525)	(411,061)	(1,408,464)	342.6%
28 Net Borrowings	3,073,898	14,538,658	(11,464,760)	-78.9%
29 Sale and Purchase of Stock	—	2,000,000	(2,000,000)	-100.0%
30 Total Capital Cash Flow	1,129,815	15,997,477	(14,867,662)	-92.9%
31 Net Cash Gain	(12,182)	30,025	(42,208)	-140.6%
32 Net Cash Margin	-0.02%	0.07%	-0.09%	-133.8%

Unaudited - For Management Use Only

Ideas to Improve Cash Flow

Amos was pleased with the list of ideas to improve the cash flow the team had created. They tossed out the ideas, and Oliver had quickly written them on the whiteboard. At the end of the exercise, the list was extensive. The group had fun, and the idea from one person triggered ideas from other team members. Some were similar, and some were duplicates, so Amos started to scrub the list. The ideas ranged from ones that could be implemented quickly to others that could take a year or more to complete. He also tried to organize the list to conform to the buckets of the Cash Performance Report. Some of the ideas could appear in multiple spots. Many of the concepts related to accounts receivables could also reverse to become ways to slow payment of accounts payables. Amos has always prided himself on paying his bills on time and living up to his word. He never would advocate violating the integrity of the organization. Instead, the company could take deposits on customers' orders to speed up the cash coming into the company. The inverse of this could be not to pay deposits on purchases to slow the cash going out of the company.

Here is the list of ideas to improve cash flow:

Cash From Sales

1. Invoice faster / Invoice more often
2. Negotiate payment terms for faster payment
3. Create a process to follow up on delinquent accounts
4. Manage delinquent accounts with super tight controls
5. Validate the discounts given and have a process to review as needed
6. Review / negotiate / challenge credit card processing fees
7. Increase prices!
8. Reposition dead / stale / old products to a new market or purpose
9. Insource collection from collection agencies
10. Find a better / more effective collection agency
11. Make deposits daily
12. Use a bank lockbox service for payments
13. Critically review customer payment history
14. Switch appropriate clients from project-based to retainer-based accounts
15. Get rid of unprofitable or break-even clients
16. Be sure your sales agreement dictates payment terms
17. Call clients five days before bills are due
18. Assign a collections owner
19. Fire bad customers
20. Encourage electronic payment rather than checks
21. Create/tighten progress billing
22. Create a layaway program

23. Create a membership fee-based loyalty program
24. Presell product and new releases
25. Have customers prepay before shipment - any percentage is better than zero
26. Ask for deposits
27. Create automatic renewals / reorders / replenishments
28. Incentives sales team based on the cash collected, not the sales invoice
29. Selling larger order sizes
30. Reduce selling points of friction - make buying from you easy
31. Increase sales by cross-selling products better
32. Partner with related offerings to create mutually beneficial cross-sales
33. Create a subscription for your product/service
34. Charge more for more expensive services relative to value created
35. Evaluate business operating hours - increase to drive sales reduced to cut the cost
36. Solve for the customer - charge more / sell more by fixing problems and creating value
37. Reduce customer churn rates
38. Streamline product offerings to reduce confusing choices
39. Have company owners and upper management call on customers personally to identify their needs

Cost of Sales

40. Review / Negotiate every vendor to be sure you have a fair price
41. Review bills to be certain the invoiced amount is the same amount received by the company

42. Review / consolidate / challenge shipping expenses and freight terms
43. Reduce inventory levels
44. Evaluate min/max & reorder points
45. Shift to smaller, more frequent deliveries
46. Sell old inventory
47. Analyze automation to be sure it is saving you money
48. Receive inventory on consignment
49. Value engineer your offering to remove costs and increase reliability
50. Flex staffing to customer demand
51. Sell unused assets, equipment, machines, and tooling
52. Use a simple checklist to reduce errors and rework
53. Outsource task and then In source the task to bring internally when demand justifies
54. Stretch payments to vendors
55. Split purchasing among multiple suppliers to keep them competitive
56. Evaluate internal controls for theft, and reduce inventory shrinkage

Operating Expenses

57. Analyze marketing spend
58. Fire the consultants!
59. Make sure professional advisors add value relative to the expense
60. Reduce office size / renegotiate rent
61. Sublease office space
62. Outsource non-critical functions
63. In-source critical functions and potentially lower cost
64. Use independent contractors instead of employees

65. Consider using part-time employees
66. Have a clear strategy for insourcing, outsourcing, employee, contractor, consultant usage
67. Evaluate computer systems to make sure they are saving you money
68. Review list of software service providers for necessity and proper service levels
69. Review user list for software providers for terminated employees
70. Review user list for software providers for employee usage - eliminate non-usage
71. Leave vacant positions open to ensure the need for replacement is real
72. Fairly eliminate weak performing employees
73. Create a retention strategy for top performers
74. Lower employee turnover rates
75. Set up an employee incentive program to generate cost-reduction ideas
76. Pay employees bi-monthly instead of bi-weekly If your state allows it
77. Reduces overtime and other premium pay utilization
78. Eliminate all overtime hours unless prior approval is obtained
79. Create a company culture of cash discipline
80. Ask managers for written plans on eliminating unnecessary expenses in their departments and other departments
81. Create a weekly or monthly cash forecast
82. Your budget does not authorize spending
83. Work with an insurance expert to consider alternative options and savings opportunities
84. Evaluate and competitively bid insurance policies
85. Eliminate automatic renewing contracts

86. Evaluate capital expenditures for high ROI
87. Negotiate early payment incentives
88. Lease instead of buy - can be done even with office plants
89. Buy used equipment instead of new
90. Evaluate company environmental impact - reducing waste lowers cost and helps the planet
91. Reduce travel cost
92. Pay flat per diem travel rate rather than unlimited meals and entertainment
93. Utilize an administrative or part-time employee instead of a messenger service.
94. Avoid penalties from late payments/bank statements fees
95. Pay your bills at the last possible moment and pay by purchasing card
96. Negotiate with vendors to hold inventory for just in time delivery to you.

Capital Structure

97. Review your bank and lending arrangements
98. Review your leases and know the buy out dates
99. Review tax strategy with an accountant
100. Analyze the use of factoring
101. Use asset-based loans
102. Finance equipment purchases
103. Establish a bank line of credit
104. Renegotiate fixed debt
105. Refinance revolving line of credit to a term loan
106. Setup a purchasing card program with your bank
107. Analyze how the company is using credit cards
108. Have existing owners invest more cash into the company

109. Seek a capital investment by selling equity to a new investor

110. Secure a long-term bank loan

111. Explore the use of venture-debt or other investor based debt financing

112. See if SBA loans are appropriate

113. Are any government grants available

114. Are their state or local government opportunity zones that could benefit the company

115. Reduce/eliminate the company dividend

Conclusion

Amos was waiting to speak at the annual company picnic. Every year since the founding of the company, Amos has gathered all of the employees and their family's for a full weekend of fun. Looking back six months later, Amos was highly impressed with how far the team had come and how fast they did it. The dismal cash performance from the prior year had fully reversed.

After the team meeting, Amos continued to work with his leaders to drive the recovery of cash in the business. Anna worked with her sales team to collect the past due to invoices and bring payments in from customers. She also began training each sales associate on how they impact the cash flow of the company. Sarah was able to negotiate inventory shifts with primary suppliers to receive smaller, but more frequent deliveries. The agreements had an immediate impact on lowering the inventories in the warehouses, and now she was considering canceling a lease on extra space sitting empty. Oliver took the materials Amos had presented during the offsite meeting and created a training program for the company. New hires learn the company's cash culture on day one. Existing employees have begun to rotate through this initial training as well. Jacob is now producing the Cash Performance Report for the team with each month's financials. He has also built a cash forecast based on the Cash Performance Report, so everyone is thinking about the future and how their individual decisions interact.

Amos and Jacob had their bank meeting and shared the Cash Performance report. They invited the banker over to the office so they could walk the plant together and see the transformation that had begun. The bank quickly approved the requested increase in the line of credit, which provided the company with some flexibility and time to fix operations.

Sales in the current year continued to increase as customers fell in love with the RX71. The changes to Accounts Receivable processes lowered the total outstanding balance even though sales increased. Inventory levels also dropped, and the value engineering efforts paid off and lowered the cost to build each robot. The company embraced the crisis and became incredibly frugal just in time. This frugality reduced operating expenses for the company.

Amos thought about all the work and effort that everyone had done. The work the robots were doing to help the customer achieve their goals. He could see the daily counter of joules performed by the robots taking big leaps now. He knew momentum was finally building.

Amos felt good about the announcement he was about to make as he sees it as an investment in the great people that make the company so successful. He knew how close the company had come to not being able to have this annual picnic. Amos shuttered to think that he may have even had to sell the company or take outside investment that could have destroyed this culture. Now he had a surprise for everyone. Oliver called Amos to the mic.

Amos delivered his prepared remarks, thanking everyone for attending, and sharing an update on the company's future product pipeline and how well the RX71 was doing. He pointed out how the company's performance was truly exceptional and how proud he was to work with such a great team. Then he added, "And one more thing, tomorrow, Oliver and Jacob are running a special payroll to give every employee a twenty-five thousand dollar bonus!"

Have a cash flow question?
Go ahead and ask Amos.

visit amos.fcf.is

and visit the Free Cash Flow Blog
at www.FCF.is

The End

About the Author

Gregory Brickner is a CFO that is passionate about cash flow. He is known for a unique perspective to problem-solving augmented by strong technical skills, to bring growth to a variety of businesses within the healthcare, technology, and manufacturing sectors.

His work experience focuses on figuring out complicated performance issues for organizations challenged to find a higher tier of growth. As a CFO, Gregory believes in the necessity and growth of free cash flow above all else. Most often, this work has been for firms on Main Street and in business units within big corporations. Both can have similar resource constraints and market issues. Regardless of the organization, every day he pushes to get things done FAST, and when you need six signatures to buy coffee, he will go nuts.

Gregory lives with his wife and children in Metro Atlanta.

www.ingramcontent.com/pod-product-compliance
Lightning Source LLC
Chambersburg PA
CBHW022051190326
41520CB00008B/776